How M[uch World] Has Improved

For Don —
I know you know how to dance! [with words!]
Barbara Vajsa Schmitz
(at the Ranch)
October 2008

Barbara Schmitz

The Backwaters Press

Also By Barbara Schmitz

The Upside Down Heart, Sandhills Press, 2002
How to Get Out of the Body, Sandhills Press, 1999
Lives of the Saints, Sandhills Press, 1997
Making Tracks, Suburban Wilderness Press, 1985

Some of these poems have been printed previously in magazines, including *Emerging Voices* and *Cokefish*. Thanks for permission to reprint here.

Backwaters Press logo designed by L. L. Mannlein,
Copyright © 1997 by The Backwaters Press
Cover artwork © 2004 by Barbara Schmitz
Author photo copyright © 2004 by Karen Wingett
All poems copyright © 2004 by Barbara Schmitz

All rights reserved. No part of this book may be reproduced in any form, except for the inclusion of brief quotations in a review, without permission in writing from the author or publisher.

First Printing, 800 copies, December, 2004

Published by: The Backwaters Press
Greg Kosmicki, Editor/Publisher
3502 North 52nd Street
Omaha, Nebraska 68104-3506
(402) 451-4052
gkosm62735@aol.com
www.thebackwaterspress.homestead.com

ISBN: 0-9726187-5-9

Printed in The United States of America by
Morris Publishing, 3212 E. Hwy 30, Kearney, Nebraska 68847

*For Bob
Again and Always*

MOTHER WALTZ

Mother Waltz	1
My Mother Takes My Wedding Picture to the Door	7
Looking for Zinnias	8
Home	9
The House	13
November Morning	14
Christmas Birds	15
All Souls' Day	16
Deciding	17
Forty Hours	18
How to Get to Plattsmouth	20

CHOOSING RED at 51

Choosing Red at 51	25
Singing	26
Making Themselves Presentable	27
Man Gets Obelisk at 55	28
Lighting	29
Turgor	30
Summer	35
Getting Groceries on Sunday Morning	36
Hoarding Dirty Clothes	37
I Had To	38
Late Adolescence	39
Fixing Myself a Turkey Sandwich	40
The Death of Pokey	42
Magic Act	43
Finishing Eli	44
Not Erotic	45
Losing Your Nerve	46
My Dear, You Must Overcome Your Paranoia	47
The English Teacher Retires	48
Exit Interview	49
The Man Who Didn't Want to Go to Bed	51
Work is Play	52
If She	53

SECOND HONEYMOON

Second Honeymoon	57
Sunday Morning	58
Husband Out of Town Thinks About His Wife	59
It's Our Anniversary	60
Her Worst Trait	61
Snowing	64
"What is it You Want?"	65
Wife Thinks About Husband's Body	66
Light in the Wedding Photo	67
Because	68
Looking South	69
Kissing by the Cake	70

AFTER INDIA

Practice	73
After India	74
I Go to the Wedding	79
In the Bus	83
Visiting the Temple	84
Drinking Cognac	85
Last Night	86
Pretty July Morning / A Little Breeze	87

HOLY HOLY HOLY

After Ginsberg	91
And So	92
Allen Remembered	93
Stupid God	94
How to Fix the Charcoal Drawing	95
How to Accept the Totally Opposite Point of View	96
Pantoum Begun With Lines From Susan Minot	97
Pantoum Two Started With Lines From Susan Minot	98
Walk	99
"Blizzard"	102
Learning to Draw Lying Down	103
Strangely Warm October Day	105
Ways to Know God	106
December 1999/Dear Natalie,	110
New Year's Day 2000/What I Leave Behind	111

How Much Our Dancing Has Improved

Barbara Schmitz

MOTHER WALTZ

MOTHER WALTZ

    1 (After the talk)

I ran
and climbed
and straddled
    the crotch of the cherry tree
    hanging on
clinging
to a thick limb
and my childhood
    girlhood
everything I knew
    to be real
    and true
Knowing now I'd been
    kicked out of Eden
and soon soon
    All of this I loved
      walking doll
      second-hand bike
      cocker spaniel
would be swept away
in the coming flood

    2

All of the time she gave in too easy
She wanted pink for her bedroom wall
She shrugged her shoulders and said then
I could have that color like sunrise roses

She always was the one to give
things up She said she liked milk
but didn't drink it so we kids
could have more
I didn't even like milk
She bought her dresses at the

church rummage store
When I got older I wished
for her to have pretty things

Our mean cocker spaniel would
follow her when she left home
She would plead and pray
but never give praise
Would never say you look
pretty that looks good
Her only fragrances were shampoo
and the whiff of white talcum powder

She lived like a nun although
she was married She would
bruise her knees from all the
floor scrubbing Her bedroom
was blue but she really wanted
pink

      3

"You're going to fry in Hell,
 for missing Mass," my mother insists,
pointing toward the glowing burner
beneath her pan of frozen chili.
She nods her chin down. "Hell
is much hotter than this."

I feel bad, not for my sin
she imagines, but for her
searing her own heart for me.
How to remove the cataracts
of dogma from her eyes,
skim the froth of concept
from her boiling brain?
How to help her see–
we're all together in the pot,
her, God, me,
stewing on her stove.

4 (We're Making Gravy)

My mom and me. It's Thanksgiving.
My dad is still alive. The cupboard
doors are still off, not yet refinished.

She's making gravy. I'm stirring
the bubbling brown sauce in
my cast iron pan. I'm supposed

to be learning. But like math
and directions I can't
learn this. I don't cook much meat.

Feel prejudiced toward gravy.
We're beaming, heads together
for my husband with the camera.

Her brown eyes, my blue.
Her black hair, my blond.
Faces open and full of light.

5

"Bring me a tissue,"
my mother says
after we both spy
a tiny turd (bird turd)
she leaves on the chair
as she dresses
from the hot tub.

"Here," she says, handing
tissue and turd to me.
"A present."
"Thank you," I say
and nod carrying both
to the toilet.
After all, I tell myself,
she changed all those
diapers for me.

I resist snatching the towel
she laid her egg on and jamming
it down the laundry chute
like a contagious small pox blanket.

I offer her my arm.

      6 (Grief)

When she died
they grabbed
her new robe
Christmas snow globe
stuffed mouse
radio
ceramic Santa
clothes
and gave
by the handsful
to the nurses
aides
all in attendance
all her belongings
away
'till like her
beneath crossed hands
closed eyes
they too
were empty skies

      7

Aunt Helen says my mother hadn't
been taking care of her hair. She'd
been using the old brush rollers
I'd left from high school in the 60's.
"Why buy new when the old'll
do just fine..."

Her attitude in me: we'd been using
the 35 dollar gas stove we got
when we first moved to town until

the busted door smacked my husband
on the head when he had to keep relighting
the pilot light again and again and he
insisted we buy a new one. Picked out
a shiny silver space-age stove with
self-cleaning oven too small for our
Thanksgiving turkey.

I want to tell Helen I like Mom's hair now.
She just washed it and left it alone, and
actually she did something *I* told her
to do; but we both just stare down at her,
And Helen says, "something's wrong
about her mouth."

      8

After dinner, my mother's finger,
points to the counter
to direct my son to scraps for the dog.
It's my voice, her gesture.

Is that where she's gone to? To live
inside me? Is that eternity?
Our ancestors stacked inside us,
like Chinese boxes, down and down,
through the centuries? A movement
here. A comment there. A familiar glance.
How much our dancing has improved!

      9

Doves cry
Blood flows in fingers
Dog turns on side
Television goes off in basement
Tires outside rolling rolling

Air conditioner turns on
Pen scratches on paper
Stomach rumbles
Sunlight flicks across carpet
Trucks shift gears

In my dream I waltz
my dead mother to bed
She wears her nightgown
that hangs in my closet
I hear her laugh
awake in the night

MY MOTHER TAKES MY WEDDING PICTURE TO THE DOOR

My beautiful black-haired, blue-eyed,
short-time high school boyfriend
stops by. Asks my mother about me.

"Married. Married. Married." My mother
chants waving the banner of my wedding
photo high above him like the landing
at Guantanamo. She doesn't tell me
until his trail's no longer traceable.

Visiting one weekend, at dinner,
in between bites of meat, she says,
"Danny was here." A thin apparition
brushing dark hair out of lake blue
eyes whisks by. My fork full of
butter beans halts in mid air.

"When? Where?" my mouth asks
while my mind travels to that
flower bud time remembering
those slanted eyes, his smile turned
up one side and how I was pretty
because he saw my tender petal beauty.

I swallow, not wanting to make him
appear before me, but not wanting
to eat any more dinner.

LOOKING FOR ZINNIAS

Not these itty bitty puny things
I say to Betty at the nursery.

Big, bright pokey ones—
the kinds with spikes—

like my father used to carry
grinning up the walk.

A tight, bright wad
clutched in his rough paw.

HOME

Getting over a migraine is coming home

Ladekh, India   The high Himalayas
Dark monastery with flickering butter lamps is home

Dreams are home   My dead mother
visits every night

Praying is home

When I was a child I longed for God—
Heaven was my home
I had been left behind

I thought I was adopted   My parents'
hard-working ways   My brothers'
football car conversations were alien

I sat on the porch summer nights,
couldn't stand air-conditioning
Night sky felt like home

The park across the street with its set
of swings, garbage can, where I
learned to ride my bide
bouncing from tree to tree

Daydreaming, drawing
in the dirt
beneath the swings
with my toe
was home

My pink rose wallpapered closet wall
warmed by the furnace duct
was home

Mary Liz's brick house across the highway
wasn't home   I wanted to go home
to my mother

on her knees
in the garden picking peas

My grandparents' houses weren't home
Grandma Hohman made us drink milk
from lumpy powder
Grandpa Koubek's house
was gloomy
with huge wooden-framed Sacred Heart
of Jesus and Mary   bleeding
They read each other the paper
in Bohemian

My mean cocker spaniel
was home
The kids at the Catholic school who
made fun of me weren't home

The Lives of the Saints, the mumbled Latin,
the smell of incense, the Stations
of the Cross were

Sunlight flitting through stained glass
of curly-haired Jesus in red,
a lamb beside him, was home

Until I was about twelve
Joy to the World after Midnight Mass
was home

My uncle's farm with his loud voice
at three big meals a day
when I'd stay in the summer
wasn't home
Maybe the sticky dusty smell
in the hen house gathering
still warm eggs in a basket

Singing is not home
Sometimes
when my mind forgets
I drop into the home

of   dancing
Sun on the neighbor's white shingles
is home

The hum of the refrigerator running
The din of the vacuum   Music
playing upstairs
Riding in a car in sunlight
is home

Quiet

Robin song   Cardinal trill
Spitz howling at ambulances

Potato salad—not too mustardy—
my mother's kind—
is home

Harney Peak after a difficult climb
is home

In the worst ghetto
in Delhi
the tomb of Inayat Khan
is home

Rumi's joyful golden lamp-hung
tomb in Konys, Turkey
is home

The Topaki Palace
in Istanbul where a priest
chants over Mohammed's remains
is home

Soft, pretty
clothes
are home

Art and art museums
are home for a few hours then

I feel ill from artists'
brush strokes
and vibes screeching
from the canvas and they are not home

My
toes
knees
hands
face
are home
My stomach
and hair
belong
to somebody else

Steps I take through my day

The conscious breaths I breathe

When I see with the eyes of compassion
everybody
everything
is my home

THE HOUSE

The house belongs to them now—
423 South 9th Street, 402-296-5087.
It hasn't been my home really
since I went away to college.

My brother cried when he turned off
the kitchen light for the last time,
after hauling a '50s buffet out of the attic,
tossing the rest of canning jars in the trash.

They bought it after we filled the cistern
with cement and had the premises
sprayed for termites. They decorated it
right away with wooden women lawn ornaments.

I only drove by once, approving of
the ceramic swans overflowing with petunias
on each side of the cement porch Dad built,
disposing of old brass bed parts in the foundation.

They wouldn't know about that
or our old childhood home ghosts
we've left behind in the dream dimension—
our lives going on much the same,
just underneath, next to theirs.

Mother's floured hands rolling out
dinner rolls while they converse at
morning coffee. My father fixing
curtain rods in the basement while
they watch football on television.

My brothers fight with snowballs outside,
cocker barking, while they shop for groceries.
And while they sleep, my sweet
girl ghost huddles in the bedroom closet
devouring page after page of *Gone with the Wind.*

NOVEMBER MORNING

Branch shadows on dining room wall.
Everybody else asleep. Oh!
Sleep On! Dream On!
From the nether world my father
bongs his homemade pipe chimes
on my front porch outside.

It's close to the November day
he died. I dream he buries
my dead body. Hefts it on
his dead shoulder. Then
we both go on down the road
in his old car. Bare tree
branches scrape the window.

Father, I remember you.
Do you remember me?

CHRISTMAS BIRDS

"Help me out! Help Me Out!"
a white-haired crone caws
in the dining room even though
the blond nurse is right beside her.

Another woman calls numbers
"54! Tom," An old guy squawks,
"54!" across the room. "58! Tom.
58!"

"What'er they doing?" I whisper
to an aide. "Counting cars,"
the answer. We spoon ice cream

into my father-in-law. "You
 know today is Christmas?"
He swallows, stares, shrugs.

"Isn't that something?"
Waits with his open bird beak.

ALL SOUL'S DAY

When I was little
this day was
more important to me
than Halloween. I
didn't care about
costumes and candy.

I *did* believe what
the nuns said about
All Soul's Day being
a special time you
could release souls
from Purgatory— that
fiery waiting place
like Hell only temporary.

They let us go from school.
I prayed all day,
envisioning white fluffy
puffs of souls soaring
upward through golden gates

unchained from flames
suffering, pain
because of me;
and someday I thought
some small child
would clasp her hands
eyes turned up
and pray for me.

Perpetual Light, Oh Lord—
whatever that was—
flooding my soul,
washing me clean.

DECIDING

I was all set—
Sister Janette quizzing me
on the concrete steps
with iron bar railing
after daily summer Mass,
"Yes," I'd thought about it.
I didn't tell her most of me
was already packed
had decided
had a pact in my mind
           my heart
             with God.

I'd go live with him
        in a cell,
pray from morning to night,
do everything right.
Then I'd get the prize,
squeeze into those narrow gates—
a camel passing
through the needle's eye.

But a little butterfly thought
fluttered just at the edge
           of my decision.
Maybe...just maybe...
I should first try high school,
see what boys were like.

I didn't go to the convent.

FORTY HOURS

Late at night,
past my bedtime,
still a small child,

once a year,
the priests from neighboring towns
marched in our Forty Hours Service.

The Host in its gold monstrance,
transparent glass where it could be viewed
"exposed" on the church altar,
for forty hours straight. Parishioners
had to sign up for an hour
to stay in the presence of "The Lord"
through the odd times of the night,
keeping him company, praying.

Special devotions,
three nights in a row.
Incense, chants, bells.

My favorite part—
The Closing.
Deep male voices
Reciting: *Santa Lucia,*
Ora Pro Nobis.
Santa Barbara,
Ora Pro Nobis.
Santa Raphael,
Ora Pro Nobis.
On and on.

My eyes drifting
under drooping lids,
down through the saints,
angels, Mary,
urging them all—
Ora pro nobis—
To pray for us—
Interchenete Pro Nobis—
To intercede for us.

The priests in their black cassocks
white surplices.
Trooping around the church.

And Jesus,
his white round bread self,
sniffing the sweet smells
wafting through the hard wooden pews,

watching us kneel about to keel over
from exhaustion and ecstasy,

witnessing all this,
from his golden container,
there on the altar,
high above us all.

HOW TO GET TO PLATTSMOUTH

It's there. Smack dab in the Midwest.
Where the Platte and the Missouri
meet and kiss and keep on moving,
chugging to the Mississippi.

It's high on hills that are hard
to climb in winter. Ice covered.
Cars and shoes sliding backward.

Oak and acorn covered.

Older than Omaha. An old
river town.

President Truman stood on
the balcony of a caboose
there: stopped for
a couple minutes. After
the war was over.

The flood waters would raise
their hips in spring . Daring
to sashay to the end of Main
Street. Almost all the way
up to the meat lockers once.

More bars per capita than
any other little town in
the '40s.

Lots of hot rods zooming
around A & W Rootbeer stand.

The high school was on top
of the hill with funny old
teachers: Margaret Kruse
who taught geometry *and*
English, Kleenex stuffed
in her low cut dress, spraying
saliva on the students in the
front row. Cecil Comstock,

hand, palm up, on his shoulder, reciting
Joyce Kilmer's "Trees." The Coach we
called "Possum" and painted swastikas
on his history room door.

South of Offutt Air Force Base,
Strategic Air Command, Ground
Zero in the '50s. A special
command center underground
where the war would be fought
in case of nuclear attack.

Safe enough for a young girl
to walk home at night after
a ball game, a dance. . . (my
father said if anyone grabbed
me, they'd let me go at
the first street light.)

It's still there. 20 miles
South of Omaha, around Dead
Man's Curve, past what used to be
Merritt's Beach. You can come
in on the highway next to the cemetery,
where my great grandparents, Czech
grandparents, uncle and aunts, mother
and father, one cousin my age
remain—silent lookouts, cherishing
Plattsmouth's fragments in their
crumbling, letting go bones.

Choosing Red at 51

CHOOSING RED AT 51

A new winter coat with black fur collar.
The first one I see,
the only one I'll consider.
I sigh at the navies, browns.
No black! I say as the clerk
carries one toward me.
She returns it to the rack.

A new skirt and sweater.
Both red.
You look good in that color!
says Becky at dinner at The Uptown.
Makes your cheeks all rosy
Claudia says. Red.

Black Elk saw in his vision
the Black Road of Difficulty
intersected the Good Red Road.
In the center was the Sacred Place.
More than halfway through my life,
I wear lipstick again lighting up
my face. I refuse to be invisible
as I move toward the dark embrace.

SINGING

I'm singing.
Some people call it aging.
I look into the mirror to laugh.
Start wearing lipstick at fifty-one.

The mirror handle is carved,
wooden, turns
and music plays.

Sometimes now, angels
let me see them walk
boldly beside me, whispering
to teach me a few spirit words.

And, oh, they comb my hair
with gold and silver brushes
weaving years of pain, years
of joy in between my own
fine strands. "Love means,"
they say, "taking care of
someone."   Singing.

MAKING THEMSELVES PRESENTABLE

It takes about an hour.

He whitens his teeth
with washes and pics.
She applies makeup she
eschewed for so many years.
Patina: the shine from scratches.
Distressed wood: new wood
hit with chains and crowbars
to give a weathered effect.

She smooths concealer over
sunspots etched in skin.
He combs hair over
the round shiny place in back.

They peer in their mirrors.
She, a full-length view
reflected from closet door.
He, a close-up under
all the bathroom light.

She sees herself at 18.
No jowls, smooth chin,
tanned glowing skin.
He sees the young man
who fell in love with her.
Blue eyes glowing
under tangled curls.

They turn to each other, touch
hands, go out the kitchen door.

MAN GETS OBELISK AT 55

He likes it. Sets it
different places at various
angles in his dining room.

Thinks he is the only person
in his town to have
an obelisk. Thinks it is
symbolic and religious but
artistic too. Forgot he said
he wanted it. Is glad to
have a surprise. Says he likes
his birthday just fine
even though his wife didn't
invite anybody over. Calls
an old friend in California.

Now it is twilight.
Almost, almost dark.
There is no light
anymore on the obelisk.
It hums silence
in the dusk.

LIGHTING

He spends the afternoon installing
halogen lights under the kitchen cupboards
above the counters. We'll have those
beside the string of white Christmas
bulbs he innovated for kitchen light years ago.

I wanted him to put away
the hot tub cleaning ingredients—
potions, bottles in a cardboard box underneath
the white wooden desk upstairs.

He doesn't quite clean up his mess,
waits for me to admire his work.
"Yes! Nice job, " I manage.
"Did I want new lights?" my mouth adds.

I'm coming down with a migraine,
know I should shut up, know I
should praise this man who lights
up every corner of my house, my life,

but some stubborn part of me wants
to sulk instead, having learned to look
at specks and grime, instead of clouds and sky.

I look him in the eye. He nods,
going about his task—giving light—
the way he wants to, the way he shines.

TURGOR

(To be swollen-in art-broken contour lines)

The sun is relentless through transparent
blinds in the afternoon bedroom

This time of day she doesn't feel
too well
nausea and ache

Sometimes is not even sure who she
is in there   watching whoever she is
out here in the mirror

Her hair flips out in back but it
is much better now than curly

She cleans her chakras and often goes
to sleep   breathing in and out   the crown
in and out   the third eye

She was taught never to cross out
erase   to write with a pen

She doesn't bother about the back
of her hair   She can't see there or
dirt in those places no one sees

Not grey today   No   That color is
not good for her   Is grey good for anybody?
More color to wear in the world than black

Thickness around the middle   Like
Clotted cream   Her soups and stews no
matter how much liquid she adds
always thicken

always thickened   used to be
a thin young thing   proud so proud

An ache at the end of her
tailbone   If she were a bird
she'd have feathers there   They
would   ache too

Contour he says   Turgor   Broken lines
Show weight shift   She doesn't know how
to do this

Relentless Relentless   Meals
planned   shopped for   Eaten

She wants to lie down   Not to
see spots on her face in the
mirror

The house creaks   The vines on
chains creak   The wind blows
always on the prairie

The blinds are blue   The floor is
green   There is no water in the hot tub

Cut zinnias do not last long
in the house these days

The car has the Service Engine
Soon sign on   The brakes have
never worked well

This thickening   Thickening
around the middle

The house cleaner will come
only every two weeks

Don't incite   Invite

The putty goes down layer by layer
onto the cracks in the shower

Chili for lunch even though it's
hot outside

A far off train whistle
A siren from an ambulance

Begin again Every day The white
page The clock hours
toenails   fingernails

Does the band music bother anyone
The yoga teacher wants to know
Door open

Wind Come In was his first poem
long ago before he lost interest
in things literary

Notebook on her stomach She tries
to doze The lines keep pouring
She'll have to turn on her side

The wind sounds like traffic

What do they see? What do they see
in the mirror he wants to know

She doesn't look in the mirror if
she can help it
Wobbly skin under chin   spots on face
Shiny   shiny eyes

The "I like my...." game   You
fill in the blanks   Hair   Eyes
Legs   There must be some other parts

Who gets the prize?

Fierce carved wooden mother with infant
in her arms   Looks full-grown

What time is the next event?

in and out   in and out   Breathing

house creaking   creaking

last night the wind wasn't blowing

57   She will be 57

She noticed the skin on her belly
looked different   Just lately
Once on a street corner in the Village
she could feel the presence of
e.e. cummings

And some people as if she's
known them before   Maybe they
are only body types

People in movies look like people
she knows

Creak   Creaking   Creaking

She got new red shoes   Red Cobra
it said on the box

Sounds like someone attempting
to open the attic door

small bone ache   little chicken bone

She has trouble turning her heart
upside down

The broken line of the contour   Turgor
Grrrr said the tiger   If I find ya'
I'll haveya' and that'll be that

Small appliance repair   Now we throw
them in the garbage   anywhere

She finds good things she says in the ditches
when she walks

small cracked bone ache   all the
marrow exiting

creaking   creaking

broken lines

to show where weight is shifting

SUMMERS

Balmy Colorado   Fragrant pinecone air
Blazing sun   Days of high altitude
Sunburn   Once I grew tiny weepy
breast blisters with my shirt off all afternoon
sheets stuck   had to be ripped away

We smelled air   smoked pot   drank beer
Tanning   reading writing by townhouse pool
Richard called me Nutbrown Maiden
Poetry readings   Word Soup   Crazy Talk
Yak Yak Yak Lectures Classes Buddhists
Writers from every state   Sitting on cushions
Buddha Dharma Sangha   Talks with guru
Rimpoche drank saki   Sometimes drunk
Every night a party   When did we write?
Friends like me   Always talking reading laughing
Making poems   Flirtations   Wine   Kisses
Short-shorts   ass-cheek exposed   Gauzy blouses
Birkenstocks   Peony in hair

Sufi dancing   Music   Climbing in meadow
Stony Peak   Looking down on red-tiled roofs of Boulder
Walking on "the Hill"   Record stores   Frye boots
Outdoor Pearl Street Mall   New York Deli
Bagels Creamcheese   Lox Matzo ball soup
Potter's tables on sidewalk Big glasses
White wine

He always did what I wanted
Took me places in our blue Van
Red paneling Red carpet   Platform
to shove things under Sleep on top of
Camped by Arapahoe Glacier
Washing in cold stream   Trying
to touch/connect   Have good sex
Blown apart by sexy New Age Boulder
Hannah Kroeger Health Food Store
Lunch three kinds of salad—beets carrots green
Eat on mall with guitars violins mimes
Someone on a soapbox   New York
spread all the way west to Rockies
Sweet clover air

GETTING GROCERIES ON SUNDAY MORNING

She goes to bed early Saturday night
so she can get to the grocery store on Sunday
before ten. Then, the multicolored stacks
of cans, cellophane wrapped cardboard boxes,
glisten under flickering fluorescent light
in early empty aisle after aisle.

Unencumbered by clogged arteries of
carts, begging kids, squalling infants,
whole farm families stopping to chat
around noon, she whizzes her soul down
gleaming linoleum paths by heart, reaching
out Shiva-like from one side or the other
tumbling napkins, toilet paper, cheese
and bread like familiar prayer on top
of baked beans and soup, old sermons.

The early morning store is hushed
like church services where sleepy
adults and squirming children wait
for the minister's drone to stop so
they can race down those hallowed
aisles straight to Hy-Vee for cookies,
a six-pack, some smokes, and cold cuts
for Sunday night supper. She leaves
her offering on the way out, hallelujahs
all the way home.

HOARDING DIRTY CLOTHES

He saves them up.
Like Midas' gold
until I plead for
dirty laundry. Then,

he lets me have it,
a two-ton truck dumped
down the old house's
three-story laundry chute.

KA-PLOP, a wad
smacks the wooden bottom.
THUMP BUMP, another arrives,
Lands on top the first.

WHOOSH. WHOOM. It gathers speed.
These begrimed jeans.
Soiled socks falling like
Icarus doomed to his fatal splash.

Last, he giggles down
this hollow house artery.
A naughty kid, not at all
sorry about spilling his milk.

I HAD TO

slice the cow eyeball
in my son's sixth grade class.
Each kid invited a parent.
I didn't want to do it either,
but *I* was the mother
like setting an example not
to be afraid of snakes, I
stood quietly as one slithered
out of the trees onto the river
road we were walking.
My son screamed and ran
the other way before I
could whisper, "Don't
be afraid. It's just one
of life's slinking perversities."

LATE ADOLESCENCE

When in doubt what to do,
she does laundry. Something balancing
about sorting piles of color, piles
of white on red concrete basement floor.

Or she cleans, shakes out her fears
over the cement back stairs with
the kitchen rugs, always dirty.
The calm comes so briefly.

Then some sudden thud startles the peace
like black walnuts smacking
the flat black roof in the night
as she lies in the hide-a-bed,

husband snoring a rhythmic storm
in their bedroom upstairs.
She thinking of rishis and mountain tops,
the saints praying in deep night.

Probably he's alright, not in trouble—
1:45. She just wishes for the sleep
that skitters just beyond her reach,
and that he'd just come home.

FIXING MYSELF A TURKEY SANDWICH

I would prefer not to eat meat—
for health reasons and to stay thin,
and I, for sure, don't want to have
to kill an animal to have a sandwich
and prefer not to think about it
walking or crawling and squawking
a short while ago like when my son
was four or five and he'd have trouble
with chicken pieces because they were
so graphic. Now he's come home to
live and go to college and he always
wants to eat meat. We made a deal
when he was small. I'd cook and eat
what he liked two or three nights
and then he was supposed to eat
what I liked a night or two, but he
never liked my meatless dishes, and
I was the cook and wanted to please
people, make then happy, make meals
they savored even though I rejected
that old way women showed their love
like my father fixing my faucets instead
of saying he loved me, but mostly
ended up cooking meat—turkey and chicken.
I would only carry this *so* far.

Now, I've got all this white turkey meat
in the fridge because my son doesn't
like leftovers and I cooked a turkey breast
and he hardly ever eats sandwiches
because I tried to make him eat wheat bread
instead of white when he was little and if
I don't eat it, it will go to waste and
my mother taught me not to waste food.
I am hungry. Everyone else is sleeping.
I wish I would have bought that black skirt
in Omaha but the black top didn't go with it
and my husband had gone on to the restaurant
because he had to go to the bathroom and
I couldn't ask him how the right size skirt
Looked—I had tried on a size too big when
he was there and I wasn't sure what I could
wear with it or if it fit good over my stomach
so I walked out without it and when I get home
the clothes I've ordered from the catalog don't
work either—the tall skirt's too long, the extra
large top the clerk on the phone talked me into
is too big and I don't like the way the linen painter's
pants fit either so I'll have to send it all back and
I could have bought that skirt.

The only thing I got done this morning
is to take a shower and wash my hair,
but the hair gel was still in my suitcase
and I forgot to go get it so my hair dried
without it and it's all soft with no scrunch
and I'll have to do it over. I need to do
some laundry, but my son is sleeping
and the laundry room's next to his,
so I guess I'll go make a turkey sandwich
with lettuce, tomatoes, mayonnaise, and horseradish.
My husband only likes bread and meat. If
I give the turkey to the dog, he'll
throw it up.

THE DEATH OF POKEY

She died while we were in the Greek restaurant
eating roasted chicken and potatoes–
having roasted herself earlier–
nearly baking herself through
in the afternoon rear car window.

My husband rinsed her in a nearby fountain.
The vet brought her almost back
with injections of coolant needled
into her half-cooked veins.

Dry glassy eyes stared up at our son,
who cried confessing he didn't
like her anymore.
Her soul leaked away
while we stopped to eat,
having explained to the doctor
we couldn't leave her overnight.
We lived 100 miles away, were only
in the city to retrieve me from a flight.

Her milky eye light faded to black
then blank.
Her basted body letting go of her spirit;
and our son howling so loud
there in the parking lot,
residents rushed out of their air-conditioning
to see who was hurt, who needed saving.

MAGIC ACT

        (for Trisha)

Walnut tree leaves scratch
their heads and rustle.
Lovely lilies have surprised
us all again.

Dancing purple and pink,
sporting streaks of blue,
all unfurled and fragrant
on their slender naked stems.

"They weren't there yesterday,"
my son's girlfriend says,
walking past the nodding row
of ravishing beauties who giggle
softly about their sudden yearly
performance.

FINISHING ELI

Yes, I know all the stuff about sons
leaving home at 18. Kicking them
out softly or otherwise—too attached
to moms. They must go, go, go...

But, oh, he wasn't ready. He
wanted to be able to get water
and ice from the new refrigerator's
automatic door. His girlfriend
was still in high school, a year behind.
He didn't like the dormitory and all
the different girls in his roommate's bed.

There were still things we hadn't
taught him—to iron a shirt, about
cooking pasta, how to start the snow
blower. What we believe about God.

And, Holy Cow! now he's listening.
Lets us finish our sentences. Even,
sometimes, asks *us* questions when he
ices his cooler and tells us where
he's going for the evening.

NOT EROTIC

The dentist is not erotic—
smell of rubber gloves
dentist antiseptic—
even when he tells me his dream
and my filling falls out at home

Cooking dinner is not erotic—
pressure, demand, get it done—
pleasing everybody's kinky predilections,
matching everybody's different tongues

Sweeping, scrubbing, scouring
the sink, toilet, tile is not erotic
nor dusting, wiping counters,
washing windows with spray

Flower arranging is a little sexy,
pistils, stamens and reds and
yellow shouting to be noticed
Soft beds of green leaves

Polishing shoes is not erotic
nor ironing, pressing wrinkles
out smooth nor plastic surgery
Bathing is nice—all that touching
of body parts, soaps, shampoos, gels

Picking up walnuts is neutral,
pleasant to be outside but no turn
on to make you juicy   Black walnut
smell remaining on your fingers

Making beds is mostly work
unless you fall into them together
afterward, snuggling, feeling wrinkle-
free sheets, silky soft skin

Praying? Maybe...
You know like, "God, oh God, don't stop..."
And, "Please, please, Lord, do it again"

LOSING YOUR NERVE

You used to remember how to
spring off the diving board,
have done it a zillion times—
even in your dreams;
but suddenly standing there
it all evaporates in summer
hot air. Your knees tremble.
You can't think how to
arrange your arms, hands
as swimmers waiting behind
get loud and pushy in their long line.

You have to bow your head, back
up, back down, go back down
the ladder the way you came—
hoping it'll all come back,
spring up again like your body
surfacing all by itself
from deep water, a ray
of light down below pointing
out the way to go.

MY DEAR, YOU MUST OVERCOME YOUR PARANOIA

(for P.K.)

You must not assume assume
the forces are malevolent—
to get you, to get you. Assume,
first of all, the universe is benign:
that meteorites will miss the earth,
that the traffic jam is not aimed
deliberately to make you late the one
last time you cannot afford for work,
the market did not intentionally stop
ordering the kind of refried beans
you always use for your burritos.

Assume instead the sun rises
every morning just for you, the seasons
dance and shimmer with heat, snow,
changing leaves, new buds for you,
that twilight is your special gift,
and dark night with its gentle
cover is yours, my worried friend.

THE ENGLISH TEACHER RETIRES

She stops by her office one last time
and there are students in a long line
waiting to hand in papers. She unlocks
the door, sighs, pulls out the chair.
Is she supposed to be a physician,
fix what's wrong with their bodies?
A psychologist, help them with
their traumas and bruised feelings?
A priest, hear their confessions
and listen to their doubts?
A psychic, foretell their bright futures
and predict happy love lives?

It's a surprise. The first one hands her
only an empty sheet of blinding bright paper.
And so does the second, the third—
The whole lengthy, snaky line.
Each one bows, smiles, and blesses her
with one white sheet. No more words
to read! No more black marks to make!
No guidance to write in the margins!
A collection of unwritten thank yous.
Passed from them, back to her.
A book with nothing in it. To hold
between her hands. To press
to her heart. To keep.

EXIT INTERVIEW

All things considered it was
a pretty good job. Summers off
and holidays—enough time to dip
however briefly into ponds of books,
streams of poems—cooling off,
lying back supported to float
and stare at sky, momentarily
covered sometimes by clouds.
But then, the clouds drifted by
and work came back and students
who didn't love books, didn't
care to read. Some even who
crossed their arms, shook their
long or short (as the years passed)
hair and grinned. Happy in their
chosen ignorance. Creatures that
no amount of tugging or pushing
could budge. I had to let loose
of sadness and move on beyond
regret and not hold to my heart
the pay measuring what I felt
I deserved against the lighter
weight of what I received.

Bosses mostly were busy with
forms and papers and making
marks which were supposed to
mean something to someone
and left me alone to wander
through desks and faces tossing
out tasty bits for those who
leap up to bite on them.

Only one or two tried to thwart
me for power or male urge
to come out ahead of a female
unless she was willing to lie
beneath . They are dead now
or moved away. And, me,
I'm going now too with some

bittersweet threaded in my fingers.

Many names I've forgotten,
most faces I still recognize.
Like coins, like water, like
anonymous gifts left
on the doorsill, some brilliance
and much feeling has passed
between us. They go on.
So do I.

THE MAN WHO DIDN'T WANT TO GO TO BED

Some deep dread of linen.
To lay his body down all
vulnerable. To let go of
Consciousness—this knowing
what everybody's doing; what
is going on in corners of his
house, block, neighborhood, earth.
His own inner movie show
inside his head, clicked to Off.

To surrender. Sink into
a land without dreams.
Give up the day—let it
float away—acknowledge
it is all used up. Kaput!
To be in a death-like state.
Absent but breathing. Not
be anymore, anything.
Asleep.

WORK IS PLAY

I'm playing at my work.
I'm working at my work.
I'm working at my work
on the front porch that needs sweeping.
(I'll do the sweeping work later
and clean the bathroom mirror).
I'm working with burgundy notebook
and black rolling ball pen.
I'm working with nuts and dried fruit
in a cup beside me (now in my belly).
I'm working with coffee and milk
in a "Starry Night" coffee mug.
I'm playing with Anne Waldman's
Fast Speaking Woman:
"I'm the vexed woman.
I'm the woman put a hex on you.
I'm the babbling woman.
I'm the baksheesh baksheesh baksheesh woman."
I don't interrupt my work/play
to pet the white spitz
puff puff puffing beside me.
I'm working to the traffic sound.
I'm playing with semi shifts,
brake squeaks, squawks and toots.
I'm praying with snatches of tunes
from boom booming car stereos.
I'm writing with the crickets.
I'm lyricizing with the birds.
My nose smells the stink of meat processing
stealing up the street.
I'm admiring the orange trumpets
on the vine of the brown trellis.
I'm drying my suntan lotion.
(I'm only wearing a tank top).
I'm writing fast before my husband
wakes and wants coffee on the love seat.
(He thinks we're retired).
I'm working.
I'm praying.
I'm playing.
The sun comes from behind a cloud.

IF SHE

If she keeps breathing
the day will open its petals
expanding to its full bloom beauty
slowly
allowing dew drops and sunrays
to linger for long moments
on the texture of its velvet side

and there will be time enough
      to read a poem
      call a friend
      shop and cook
      go to a party
and smile

smile
at the sunbright moment
grown so large she and all the time
she wishes for slip unnoticed inside—
peering out, hands pressed against
the crystal bead of moment's side
peering at the slow motion movie
of her long long life passing by

Second Honeymoon

SECOND HONEYMOON

In a mahogany suite close to Central Park,
we could see blurry lovers in their penthouse.
We ate stringy mangoes, golden tendrils wrapping
around our teeth and holding tight.

We stayed up late to take the subway
to the Village, smoky jazz bar crowded
with New York people, bare summer clothes,
bartender rattling off beer names we didn't know.

We asked for the first kind of beer and
stayed halfway through the second band.
We left our rings and gold chains behind
in our suite, expecting too much from
them, a report they couldn't give on
the penthouse two's juicy love session.

SUNDAY MORNING

but I'm humming The Moody Blues'
"Tuesday Afternoon" while I snip
the last of the white, pink, scarlet,
fluffs of flowers named peonies from
the driveway bushes. It's overcast.

I add babies breath and bright red
roses from the bush climbing the brown fence.
I put on my black linen dress because,
well, it *is* Sunday and we *may*

go out for coffee, but probably we
won't, and I'll arrange these bouquets;
bringing more beauty into beauty
of plants, paintings and lots of light
through house's sixty-five windows.

We could use music which we neglect
these days and, oh, a gazebo and more
gardens outside and a few more friends
would be nice. But, this *is* earth.

"Swing Low, Sweet Chariot, coming for
to carry me home." Sometime. Planet's
too brightly imperfect to abandon just
yet.

HUSBAND OUT OF TOWN THINKS ABOUT HIS WIFE

He hopes she is
sitting in sunlight,
listening to Bach.
He knows how much
she likes it in their house
her house, all by herself.

What he doesn't know is:
she and the house in late afternoon
long like the cottonwood leaves
and banks of the river
for the last lingering sun fingers.
For him. For him.

IT'S OUR ANNIVERSARY

We grin so wide at
each other pearls, old coins,
roses and rubies spill
out of our lips. Together
we dance a soft shoe
to "Tea for Two" twirling
our chartreuse canes. You
in a glittering top hat; me
in red, white, and blue
satin shorts. Then the sky
opens up so the angels
can get a glimpse of us
pedaling off into the
summer night on our
bicycle built for two.

HER WORST TRAIT

Sleep
but she likes to dream

Sleep
but what else is there
to do at night?

Sleep
Reading in bed is the intention

Sleep
He is far away
watching TV
playing the piano
snacking

Sleep
She does not inhabit her body at night
Her mind has devoured all
her flesh and bone

Sleep
Actually she is praying

Sleep
She is waiting in bed
for him to come
He has to do
so many things

Sleep
Only closing her eyes
for a moment

Sleep
She was reading, honestly!

Sleep
The walnut tree
stands silent sentinel

out the bedroom window

Sleep
The moon is full
this morning in the dark

Sleep
Lately the tree has
a Hindu face and crooked arms

Sleep
It's the dreams she loves
far away travel
dead parents
initiations into Zen and Native American cults

Sleep
She always feels better
in the morning

Sleep
Her mind and body
paralyzed at night

Sleep
Never has she had
to count sheep

Sleep
She worries she won't
get enough

Sleep
Her teacher says it's
only a concept

Sleep
All screwed up
when she travels

Sleep
She arises
mourning dove
cooing on her lips
waiting
waiting for the sun

SNOWING

huge wet flakes
seen only once
or twice a season

snowing

to "Moonlight Sonata"
my mate is playing
on his new black
Yamaha in the back room

I stand at the window
hardwood floor amplifying
the piano's multilayered
lonely song

counting the snowflakes

warm shelter, music,
baked sweet potatoes,
grilled salmon almost ready

"WHAT IS IT YOU WANT?"

This afternoon. This Sunday in September.
Hot soup of summer cooling. Cooling
to chilly morning, warm afternoon softness.
Pulling weeds from what's left of flower beds:
daisies cut back, zinnias hot flashes
of pink and nearly orange. Coleus giants
bullying out everything else next to the house.

Occasional locusts, washed red
front porch. Husband echoing,
like he does through my days and dreams,
on the roof cutting back trumpet vine.

White dog.
Azure sky.
Grey pants rolled to calf,
deciding I won't cook tonight.

Like trying to find more sins to tell
the priest in childhood confessional,
there's nothing—
clear white page—
nothing else to name.

WIFE THINKS ABOUT HUSBAND'S BODY

His stomach goes flat, then blooms out again
like a deflated and blown up air mattress—
losing weight and gaining it back again.
"If you wouldn't eat crackers in bed,"
she says. He nods. "It's all the stuff
you eat at night." He smiles,

goes straight to his bin below
their two Panda bears, pulls out two kinds
of sugar-free cookies—raisin oatmeal
and almond, Harvest Crisp seeded crackers,
Honey Mustard pretzel pieces. "Chinese torture,"

she calls it, squeezing her eyes tight on her
pillow, turning on her side. The munching,
crunching amplified louder even than
the television—some scientist reporting
by how many thousands of miles the meteorite
will miss the earth twenty-two years from now.

How will she get to sleep? She invites him
to come into her dream. Maybe he'll be
lighter there, more soft. Maybe the dream'll
be dark and quiet and they can doze intertwined—
no buzzing, humming, chomp, or snore—
angels wrapped in each other's wings.

LIGHT IN THE WEDDING PHOTO

Pouring all around them.
It was the second time.
The first time was 25 years earlier in
the Catholic Church.
Their spiritual teacher marrying them
this time said the first one didn't count.
This one was the real one.

He (the teacher) was barefoot.
She (the bride) wore a crown of wild flowers
and borrowed a blue silk shawl.
The groom wore a grey t-shirt with
the globe of the earth on the back. *This
Is It* stitched in red over his heart.
They were camped in a park.

She cried with ecstasy.
She cried with joy and
the light poured down like
honey on the tableau of wedding.
On their ritual of marriage.
He (the groom) in his golden curls,
      still curling.

Both of them a little more round,
   a little more soft.
Knowing now these many years
later a little more about loving
and being blessed from the heavens—
a wedding gift—golden showers
from above. A little bit illuminating.

Light. Rays of love.
   Triangles of blessing.
Over their little wedding scene.
Caught even forever for the
scrapbook pasting   in the photograph.
LOVE   LIGHT   LIGHT
            LOVE

BECAUSE

Because it was spring; school was over for the summer.
It was sweet mock orange blossom air.
Balmy for April, the campus quiet.
He was a stranger, but not really.
I wanted the evening to go on and on.
We said we would write letters in July and August.
I would climb out that dorm window over and over.
Because he had blond curls.
Because he was my destiny.

LOOKING SOUTH

He is looking
South
out the window
the new piano
is in
He is leaning
on the windowsill
I am leaning
on him
We are waiting
for the neighbors
whose house
used to be
about where
we are looking
Now it
is
Walgreen's
parking lot
We've let
the bushes
grow high
and shaggy
for privacy
We still
like it
here
even though
the neighbors and
their house
have gone
and it
is noisy
Our lives
go on
just
about
the same
anyway

KISSING BY THE CAKE

in Hy-Vee grocery store.
For all they know
it might be Paris—
in a patisserie,
gazing down at the chocolate.
Eyes glazed over with the sugar of love.

They are young,
dark and light—
a couple who for this moment
the world is magic,
beautiful inside its glass case.

They can't see the arguments,
hear the accusations,
feel the sting of the slap,
or taste the salty tear.

For all they know
it might be Venice
and they are waiting entwined
for the gondolier to appear
to row them off into
their blissful Everafter.

After India

PRACTICE

"Practice for dying," I joked
with my editor before going
to India. The first night
I find a lump in my breast.
In the dark, trying not to wake
my mate, I enumerate all the things
I've done that I wanted to accomplish:
had a book published,
raised my kid,
been married 32 years—
but a voice inside
whimpers anyway...
" I don't *want* to die."

AFTER INDIA

After India took my notebook
After the laundry in Srinigar ruined my blue dress with scorch
   marks
After we spent all our money on shopping and tips
After we fell in love with the kids
After we woke every day at 4 a.m. to Call to Prayer and our sleeping
   was screwed up with the time change and we were so tired
   we had to nap in the afternoons
After dahl and curry, mutton and roast chicken, spinach, panere
   (cheese), flat bread roasted over the fire with strawberry
   preserves, omelets every morning, the endless stream of
   vendors on their chicharas to the houseboats—"Excuse me,
   Sir, Madam, would you like to buy flowers, postcards,
   jewelry, linens, I am a tailor"
After floating through lotus pads and buds opening into huge pink
   flowers, Habid, 70 years old rowing four adults and their
   luggage
After streets with small Indian taxis, scooters, bicycles, a cow
   meandering across at the light
After dripping wet even our underwear, 115 degrees in Delhi
After soldiers, machine guns, bunkers, and patted down body
   searches
After leis of marigolds in Delhi, leis of bachelor buttons in Srinigar
After packing, repacking, eye-identifying luggage—sure it gets in
   the taxi, on the bus, checked in at the plane
After the Baste, worst ghetto in Delhi, little kids with puffed bellies
   standing in line with their cans for milk at the Hope Project
After Suzanne holds the babies, their young mothers come for
   classes on nutrition and how to stay well, learning not to
   drink the water out of ditches
After the pool of sewage in front of Murshid's tomb
After the Paradise inside Inayat Khan's tomb, floors of marble, tree
   growing through the roof, Bliss radiating from his
   gold-covered casket
After Christ's Tomb—Who's in here?—two bodies? Huge footprint
   in cement, Baba prays out loud
After kids follow us wherever we go, gleeful and curious, wanting
   "one pen"—we give a couple, create a riot with kids hanging
   on the side on the taxi

After our teacher refuses to go in the mosque because the women cannot go and Baba, the Turkish sherif, mugs with the children, Bob teaches them the word "awesome"
After Coke which must be drunk right there so bottle can go back in the wooden carton
After winding walled streets of Srinigar, sewage running in etched cement channels
After chai and biscuits
After our houseboy names Bob, Baba, and walks into our bedroom at night to put things in the cabinet
After fields of purple flowers in Gulmarg in the Himalayas
After trekking to the top of the mountain, panting at 14,000 feet in my clogs, jamming my toes in my shoes on the way down, slowing everyone else
After Debra tries to help me and I fall in the mud
After the horsemen follow us thinking we will get tired
After a coke in base camp halfway up, we meet the others who rode horses, guides hanging onto their tails
After cheese, water, bagels on the top
After dancing, praying, chanting for Peace, Peace, Peace for this land and the horsemen saying, "You came all this way to pray for peace. It isn't even your country."
After a fire in stove in our mountain room
After burnt birthday cake and singing "Forever Young" on guitars in the Highlands Park Lobby
After walking with Abdul the guide we don't need but he needs the money
After pictures with the Hindu family at the sweet red temple
After leaving a picture of my son and his girlfriend on the temple bell at the Shiva Temple
After having a red dot put on my forehead in the steamy temple inside, a flower-decorated lingam in the center
After I leave two American dollars and get half a bag of Prasad (sweet blessed popcorn)
After Bob leaves his hat and Sabina leaps like a mountain goat up the 150 steps to retrieve it
After moonrise from behind the Himalayas, Call to Prayer floating over the water, on top of our houseboat in Srinigar
After Bill Elliot tries to explain the conflict—Kashmir sees the Indian army as an army of occupation
After buying a vajra, bronze mask, statue of Sita in Ladekh shop

After taking off my metal bracelet the last morning—knowing this
    part of my life finished, that I must leave it behind in India,
    giving the bracelet to Carmen for her daughter
After diarrhea the last morning
After Bob vomits on the way to the airport
    Security check through all our baggage
    Women soldiers looking at all my sketches and giggling
    Bob giving away two cigarettes, two candy bars, a
    peppermint to get his medicine through the checkpoint
After roses all over Murshid's tomb in the dargah, Shahabuddin's
    sweet singing, my pens exploding, Shahabuddin reading the
    ink on my hands
After all dressed up we sit in a room with the bride in red and gold
    splendor, rings and bangles on her fingers and arms, women
    singing and drumming, "Soon your husband will come and you
    will be so happy," the senile grandmother sticks out her
    tongue and lays her head on my shoulder
After we eat in groups of four: huge platter of rice, the cook adds
    morsels one at a time on top from his huge kettle—mutton,
    meatballs, cheese, intestines, we eat with our fingers, they
    videotape us and interview us—"How do you like Kashmir?
    Have you eaten food like this before? Do you like this
    food?"
After Asalam brings Bob a beer at the wedding—"They won't know
    what it is"
After the houseboat keeps moving even though it isn't when I've
    taken my malaria pills
After Shahabuddin tells me there's lots of dark forces here my
    anger isn't personal
After our "family" meals—Suzanne and Karl, Nancy and Casey, me
    and Bob around the embroidered tablecloth table in our
    houseboat—beans, cauliflower, squash, chicken, fish, boiled
    potatoes with parsley, Basir asking if we want more
    We take turns leading grace
After Nancy asked if we changed a lot since Bali—she had a
    different impression of us then
After Nancy's nose piercing and infection
After dark Corey beautiful in her flowered dress at ancient Mogul
    gardens, old roses dating from the time of King Akbar
After Zia weeps at musicians in the dargah, reaches for money in his
    gold vest pocket, touches it to the tomb and shuffles it
    trembling and bowing to the musicians over and over

After fried eggs on white bread in the Hope Project, dripping wet
    and devastated from the poverty, Shahabuddin and I split
    the last sandwich
After lunch back at the $400 a night Imperial Hotel, marble floors,
    12 foot ceilings, antique carved furniture, "Sir'ed"
    and "Madame'd" down the hall
After drinking beer in the lounge with Karl and Suzanne, band
    playing old Beatles songs, trying to explain to 19 year-old
    Nathan Beatles coming to India and meeting the Maharishi
After lunch in opulence after the Baste, weeping at "Unchained
    Melody" on grand piano in dining room, the
    dichotomy of delicious food we cannot finish
After Baba's sweet round face and hand over his heart, he doesn't
    speak English
After praying in empty canopied space at the wedding with Baba,
    "The Americans are praying!" quips Shahabuddin
After buying papier-mâché boxes, scarves, shawls
After guys on the street try to buy Bob's binoculars
After a beggar girl follows us on the street for blocks and won't go
    away
After the merchants in boats try to sell us jewelry, papier-mâché,
    tonkas as we sail to the gardens
After I get left behind for shopping, Shafee tells us to go sit in
    front of the boat and relax, doesn't want us to wait in the
    back for the taxi or buy from other merchants where he
    doesn't get a cut, he wants us to look at his rugs, "I'm not
    buying rugs," I say, "I don't need any"
After I yell at Asalam about being left behind
After we order cotton outfit in white like Shafee's and they come
    the last day in blue polyester
After the blister on my toe from the Himalayas in my clogs
After zikir and prayer and dinner and song
After Jesse's What-Color? Eyes?
After Amber's popeyed stare
After Gary works polarity on my migraine
After Sabina's songs
After buses with no air-conditioning and fans that don't work
After flowers in our houseboats
After Nathan playing soccer with the Indian kids
After kids splashing and swimming to us in the water
After the women in their new blue dresses and shawls
After the taxi drivers say they haven't had a fare for two weeks

After I know I had my notebook all the way to Amsterdam and now
	it's just missing
After the prayer wheel flies out of my hand and bams two dents into
	my coffee table at home
After all this
After all this sitting up in bed, we watch the 4th of July fireworks
	explode over our heads—grand finale a mile away at the
	lake—and dream of wars, while firecrackers crack across
	Nebraska night

I GO TO THE WEDDING

I go to the wedding
I go in beige
It's pretty
got embroidery
   but arm's not quite long enough
   pants a little too short

I go to the wedding
   Those five women all have
   fancy silky blue gowns
   "Where you get those?" I pout
   "No one showed me."
"A store on a side street," they say
while we were waiting for them for lunch

I go to the wedding
 in the white chiffon scarf silver trim
           Anna made me buy
"I don't know," I say, shaking my head
 (It only cost five dollars)
 but shopping's hard for me
 can't make up my mind
 worry about spending money
 here I don't know (rupees)
 how much I'm spending
"Just give me the money," she insists
"I'll buy it for you"

I go to the wedding
 in my new blue Birkenstocks
 thought they would match
 my lapis necklace
 but you have to fasten the straps
 and I have to keep taking my shoes
      on and off
 off to go in the main room
 on to walk the halls to where
      the bride is
 off to go in the bride room
 on to walk back to the main part

         of the house
   I give up   leave them off
   walk by where the caterers are
   pounding 40 sheep into sausage
   Servants scold me, "Where are your shoes!"

I go to the wedding
   slam my new scarf in taxi door
               make a hole
   pose for a picture with Vena
   She's young and pretty in red
   striped dress   Puts her head
   close to mine

I go to the wedding
            It's not really a wedding
   The women all sit in a room and sing
   play drums   Bride changes her clothes
                    over and over
   They sing, "Soon your husband will come
               and you will be so happy"
   The senile grandma
              hangs onto me
              sticks out her tongue
              puts her head on my shoulder

I go look for my husband at the wedding
   He's hanging out in the courtyard
               with the men
               smoking
   They bring tea
       I sit with him
       We drink Lipton's
       Kashmir tea's like soup
       I eat three biscuits

I go to the wedding
           We go upstairs
              go shopping
              buy more papier-mache boxes
              a bowl with brass inside

Come down to do prayers with Baba
    in open space under canopy
    two lines

    men in front
    women in back
    shoulder to shoulder
I don't know the movements
    do what Baba does
    It feels good
    It makes me happy

I go to the wedding
    big room
    Anna stares at me
    "You're staring at me," I say
    "You're so pretty," she says
    I glommed on more of
        the same makeup I wore all day
        Didn't know what else to do
        to be dressed up

I go to the wedding
    They bring silver pitcher
            with water
   We wash
      dry hands on towel
   get in groups of four
   around large plate of rice
   on white cloth spread on the floor

Cook with huge silver pot
    ladles one at a time
    meatball
    cheese
    intestines
Family with videocam records us
    going to the wedding
    scooping up rice with our fingers
    chewing and chewing
"You like this food?"

"Have you ever eaten food like
                    this before?"
"Do you like Kashmir?"

Finally we are through
They take the plate away
Say, "You have eaten nothing!"

I go to the wedding
         wash hands
            This time with soap

I go to the wedding
       lie on the floor
         (no furniture in Indian houses)
I'm too tired to wait for henna
           on women's hands
Eight of us cram into car
Shafee has to let us in his gate
We wander across soccer field in moonlight

I go to the wedding
I go home

IN THE BUS

We're in the bus—
coming back to Srinigar
from lovely lilac-flowered retreat,
high in the Himalayas.

There's no air conditioning,
the little mounted fans don't work.
We can slide the windows open,
but it's unseasonably hot in Srinigar.

It's a feast day—
The day they hold the tooth of Mohammed up
for believers to view in the mosque.
The streets are clogged.

Cars, taxis, rickshaws, vendors, families,
all combine to make traffic stop.
Sweat trickles between my breasts.
(I hardly ever sweat).

We pant
and sit
and wait
and breathe.

We breathe in dusty noise.
Breathe in honking, jampacked,
wavy, heat wave dream—
of dripping, dirty, Indian streets.

VISITING THE TEMPLE

We could see the temple from our cabin door.
We didn't need a guide.

He wanted to guide us. He needed money.
My husband felt sorry.

La illah illallah. I didn't want to spend
the cash; wanted us to be alone.

He showed us his license from the British
days. He liked the British. Met President
Wilson once.

We argue by the feather tick inside. He
waits outside watched by the Himalyas.

He trails behind as my husbands asks
... to keep the peace.

The temple is tiny, red, garish.
Hindu images inside glassed-in door.

We sit and meditate. An Indian
family asks us to be in their photo.

In a nearby British cemetery we read
tombstones of those who died far from home.

Dark-eyed man watches from behind trees and tombs.
My anger melts returning across rocky meadow.

Guide asks for whole day's fee—
we agree, pay him half.

DRINKING COGNAC

We're drinking cognac in the Amsterdam Airport.
It's seven in the morning on the airport clock,
but our tired bodies tick nighttime hours.

We drink beer we order in the beach
theme bar and sit at little tables high
above the airport crowd. Anything goes!

We've bought cognac, chocolate, cheese,
at the duty-free shops. Eating sweet rolls,
cheese chunks, devouring candy—all

dietary prohibitions forgotten, routines
all screwed up. We're broken-hearted
lovers wrenched away from beloved India—

Love we've met only briefly, fell for
deeply. Winging our way home now
far in the opposite direction like

bird flocks changing season.
Oh India! You remain, shrouded
in your misty Himalayas, vibrating

with color and car horns, wrapped
in the scent of strong spices, emanating
brown-eyed smiles and signaling

with little whiffs of human excrement.

LAST NIGHT

Last night in Bali we dress for temple.
It is the wooden one where the River Spirit lives.
"Isn't this far out?" laughs my guide
wrapping his bright sari around his middle.
We are going to say goodbye and must
wear the proper clothes. The women
carry the offering, sculptured fruit, on top
our heads; but we have to use our hands.
The priestess takes our flowers from folded
fingers, sprinkles us with water and gives
us a piece of rice to attach to our foreheads.
"That's all?" my young son asks, surprised.
"No sermon?" "That's it." Goodbye too:
white lotus blossoms on temple ponds; tiny
chicken cut in odd angles for dinner; bamboo
and rice offerings left on the ground, eaten by
dogs and chickens; roar of Indian Ocean;
fisherman lights on dark night waters; evening
and morning baths in river, palm trees, coconut
trees, vibrating flowers and clothes that match;
bamboo furniture and thatched roofs; rain each
night on blue plastic; cows that look like deer;
open faces, open hearts of smiling dark-eyed
muscled people who are rumored to have
descended from the tribes of Atlantis.

PRETTY JULY MORNING
A LITTLE BREEZE

God walks across the street
       chubby frumpy hair a mess
       clutching her McDonald's sack
God stops his U-Haul truck
       at the four-way intersection
       leaving town
God bawls out his cow voice
       loaded on a cattle truck
       on his way to market
God shedding white spitz
       pees on the day lilies
God rotates his arms
       round and round
       a practical dervish
       watering the lawn
God shifts down for the traffic light
       Highway 81   on the corner
God chirps a sparrow song
       answers with a cardinal cry
       murmurs soft tire prayers
             on the pavement

God sits two coffee cups on rotting
       used-to-be-red picnic table
God spills out of the whiskey barrel
       scarlet petunias
       and over-bloomed garlic
God sits in the shade
God is a busted wooden Bali chime
       hanging on bent rusted clothesline pole
God makes leaf shadows on
       brown backyard wooden fence

Little walnut tree leaf rustle
Air-conditioner kicking in

Oh God   my God
What a wondrous ordinary morning!
What a beautiful extraordinary day!

Holy Holy Holy

AFTER GINSBERG

Holy! Holy! Holy! Holy!
Chicken Soup is holy.
Pen scratching on
white paper is holy.
Early cold weather
in November, holy.

White spitz moving
from rug to rug to
be close to his family.
Son and girlfriend
happy in the basement.
The colleague at work
who feels cheated—
others got more of
something than him.

Brilliant autumn sky,
stark tree branches,
drainage in the throat.
Another migraine coming.
Holy! Holy! Holy!

AND SO

And so it is morning   Is summer
Is cloudy   Is cool
Traffic sings outside the window
A Thursday in June

Garden's late but finally planted
Daisies blooming   Peonies finished
Vines tangling themselves around
fence's throat   Up trellis' thigh

Baby sparrows flown still hover
close to nest home
Cheep Cheep   Cheeping insist
I am here   Here   This day

Dog declines open door
Plops on swept kitchen floor
He sniffs at Winter I can't see
I bow to silent broom in corner

ALLEN REMEMBERED

> *Never sat/on bed with him/*
> *never that close/ though once*
> *he kissed my lips*
>
> Ferlinghetti   "Allen This Instant"

1
Yeah, I guess he kissed me
once too
on the lips
A year or so after I'd been his apprentice
in Boulder   At some event at Naropa
I went up to him to say Hello
He took my hand and kissed me

The next time I saw him
I was holding my baby
He kissed him too

2
Once after I had taken acid
and climbed the Flatirons barefoot
All the lights from cactus spears
shot out like white fire so
I never stepped on anything sharp
Allen came to me in the parking lot
Started to rub my feet
"What 'cha been doin'?" he asked
his eyes twinkling

Told me to meditate, take LSD
I'd go into the Great Void
I was on my way home to Nebraska
Told him I *lived* there in the Void

STUPID GOD

Stupid God, made full moons
and people and dogs to go crazy
and howl at them

Stupid God, gave women
hormones to ride them up
and down like an elevator
gone wild or whinnying
wild mares captured and
their nostrils wired shut

Stupid God, made people
want children and tricked
them into thinking a little
child would grow up
to be like its mom and dad

Stupid God, decided
to experience suffering
through its creation

Stupid, Stupid, God
You never know when
to quit Twist your
own arm just a little
tighter "How like
you this?"

Yowling, yowling at
the big white ball moon

HOW TO FIX THE CHARCOAL DRAWING

Boldly. With heavy dark outlines.
Work area by area. Fill in the sky,
the grass. Make the sidewalk
bumpy. Push down hard on tree
bark. Confident contour on the garage
roof and neighbor's house. Make
the shadows black. Draw what's
there. No concepts. (Also, this
is the way to get enlightened.)

HOW TO ACCEPT THE TOTALLY OPPOSITE POINT OF VIEW

Don't panic.
Keep breathing.
Sit still as a rabbit
before it bolts for safety.
Watch the sky.

Do not try to explain your perspective.
Do not assume you are correct.
Don't draw lines through other's words.
Wash your ears.

Softly, like a mist rising over the river,
leave your body and creep
into the other's heart and mind.
Blink your new eyes.

PANTOUM BEGUN WITH LINES FROM SUSAN MINOT

"Something was dawning on her soul"
"The world was perfect, and tight, and balanced."
Mid-summer green made a humming noise.
And the cardinal started to trill when she walked outside.

The world was perfect, and tight, and balanced.
She practiced standing on one leg, lifting her arm wings.
And the cardinal started to trill when she walked outside.
The sky sat in her blue dress, still and waiting.

She practiced standing on one leg, lifting her arm wings.
Her head tilted to one side as she tried to smell God.
The sky sat in her blue dress, still and waiting.
Her childhood nuns gazed down from Heaven's edge.

Her head tilted to one side as she tried to smell God.
Mid-summer green made a humming noise.
Her childhood nuns gazed down from Heaven's edge.
Something was dawning on her soul.

PANTOUM TWO STARTED WITH LINES FROM SUSAN MINOT

"It was as if someone pierced her chest."
"If she didn't remember these things who would."
The kitchen clock did its tick-tock dance.
The dog had been gone almost eight weeks.

If she did not remember these things who would.
Her mind was a colorful album of saved dreams.
The dog had been gone almost eight weeks.
The roses and daisies were cut back to their stems.

Her mind was a colorful album of saved dreams.
She stretched her neck to the right, then the left.
The roses and daisies were cut back to their stems.
Summer's heat was attacking the marigolds.

She stretched her neck to the right, then the left.
The kitchen clock did its tick-tock dance.
Summer's heat was attacking the marigolds.
It was as if someone pierced her chest.

WALK

Walk daily
or as often as possible
swing yer arms
        back and forth when you walk
Walk fast
Walk uphill some if possible
Feel the pull at the back of yer leg
"Power walking is good for the thighs"
Do breathing practices while you walk

IN THROUGH THE NOSE   OUT THROUGH THE MOUTH
IN THROUGH THE MOUTH   OUT THROUGH THE NOSE

Walk past the hospital where yer son was born
Walk past your doctor's office
Wave to Paul if he's in his yard
Walk past the nursing home where
your father-in-law and your mother died

Walk past peoples' flower gardens
        if summer
Notice flowers you'd like to plant
Walk in the cold and dark if it is winter
Watch out for icy sidewalks!

WALK WALK WALK WALK
IN THROUGH THE MOUTH   OUT THROUGH THE NOSE

Try to think positive thoughts as you walk
Breath in and out the chakras
    Start with the crown
      Then the temples   third eye
      throat heart stomach
        Work down to the pubis
          In and out the hands and feet

Chant mantras while you walk
Not Oh, Lord I am not worthy
Ya Ghani Let me be self-sufficient
Ya Muktakabir Let me be a large person

Alahoakabar   God is Greater
Estafirla   Forgive me
Ya Sami   Ya Basir
Inner Sight   Inner Sound

Notice position of the sun
Clouds or not in the sky
Moon's visible too in early summer

ESTAFIRLA

Smile and say hello to joggers,
         bikers, other walkers as you
         round the lake
Nod to Korean nuns in white habits

GOD IS GREATER   GOD IS GREATER

Stop in cemetery
Visit Reed   suicide at 15
       Marty   cancer at 49
       Roger   heath problems all his life

ALAHOAKABAR
ALHOAKABAR

Walk past Dennis' house
         Greet him if he's outside
         Listen to his "Un, Un"
         All he can say now after his stroke

ALHOAKABAR

Walk past Brian's
         Ask him about stock market
         if he's outside

YA SAMI   YA BASIR

Notice grumpy Fred's, the custodian's, lawn
         full of rose bushes, geraniums in pots,
         phlox in barrels, wooden ornaments,

    hanging fire hydrants, beaded chimes

ALAHOAKABAR

Get barked at by dogs while cutting down alley

NICE DOGGIE   NICE DOG

Walk past adolescent 24 hour supervised home
      with drapes pulled tight
        Where are they?

IN THE NOSE   OUT THE MOUTH

Admire two story yellow house
      fence weighted down by vine
        orange flowers trumpeting

ALHOAKABAR

It's your house!
Walk inside the gate
Open front door
Call, "Honey, I'm home!"

YA SAMI   YA BASIR

"BLIZZARD"

Summer mornings the spitz
would appear on the front porch—
me settled in with coffee, books,

notebook—and like a familiar prayer
both ask and receive: blessing
me, wanting petting, and then

lie—stunning white, against red
porch floor—quiet as still life
but breathing steady, rhythmic.

God pouring from his heart and
lungs. "Good dog."

LEARNING TO DRAW LYING DOWN

(For Isabella Threkeld)

Draw sunrays to your heart
Earth embraces to your spine
Draw ants and other small black bugs
 to your body warmth
Bible warns, "Do not eat swarming insects"
Oh no, no, no, no, no, no

Draw moonbeams from sailing crescent
Clouds floating into eyes
 obscuring moonlight
 casting shadows onto your future

Draw daydreams and phantasmagorical
 visions of creation
Draw memories
 sadness of old lives
 a few sorrows left behind
 floating free

Draw the lub lub lubs of your heart
 not so active in this position
Draw the glances of curious passersby
 What is that woman doing?
 Is she drunk? Is she ill?

Draw on the remembrance of Chagall painting
 "The Poet Reclining" in mauves and greens
 grass, barn, sky
 body outstretched but grounded
 in this painting
 no souls floating Heavenward to God

Draw with crayons   pencils
 your most favorite black Pilot
 Precise V Fine Rolling Ball Pen

Draw on all past experiences
 past and present fears

with fine penmanship
encouraged with prayers and cheers

Draw out of boredom
 in sunlight
 twilight
 darkness

Draw with humor
  little balloon jokes
  floating up out of prostrated bodies
                              below

Draw to discover something
  Columbus kissing the shores
     of the new world
  Natives lying deep down in the brush
  drawing doubt about what this discovery
     means to their lives, their world

Drawing with hope
  merry little faces of souls
  yet to be incarnated
  to enter a body
  Entering the world through
  their mother's bodies
   lying on hospital table

Each new life drawing a breath
Before lying down in a transparent crib
Drawing conclusions from new born eye observation
   "So this is the world. . ."
   "So this is life. . ."
   "I'm not going to take this lying down. . ."

STRANGELY WARM OCTOBER DAY

The tiptop
of the neighbor's tree
is turning to love.
"Turn to love." "Turn to love."
the sparrows on the back roof squawk.

God loves these little creatures
As well as as well as the cistern
in the backyard, deep
dark sounds of love.

And swish, swish, swish
the sprinkler sprays green light
on the raised hands
of the grass blades.

"This Is Not My Body,"
says the brown fence,

and the clouds, the clouds
just move like thoughts
all over our blue faces.

WAYS TO KNOW GOD

Deepak Chopra wrote a book about it,
but I couldn't get past the first few pages.
Religion is supposed to be a way,
but it is mostly commands, rules, regulations.
Churches are supposed to provide a place,
but they are expensive edifices.
Stained-glass works sometimes—
filtering in colored breath of God,
but pews separate,
music can drag,
priests and preachers harp on,
painting flame and sizzle.
People check out the congregation
to see what everyone is wearing.
And churches always need more money.

There's devotion—bhakti—adoration
of the holy, a guru, God itself,
a two-way love mirror;
and yoga stretching stretching
apart the physical plane of the
body to open enough space to
let enter the Divine.

Prayer is a way, but it's hard
to get beyond the asking stage:
"Oh Lord, give me this—
I need that"
and enter a quiet place
of simply venerating glory,
light, power of God.

Meditation takes a lot of practice,
sitting still without squirming,
watching thoughts strut and prance
across the sky of your mind.
To bow, acknowledge them and
watch them exit, stage left,
unclouded mind for awhile.
And those empty spaces

when you are not there at all
are supposed to be the ones when
God comes.

The Buddhists have the Wheel of
Life and karma and time turning
around and around. Endless
suffering because of attachment.
Need right thinking. Right livelihood.

Chanting mantras—qualities of God—
is supposed to be a way.

It's hard not to be angry
and demanding.
"Well, where *is* He?
I have been waiting.
My desire is strong:
my heart is true.
Where is this Holy Grail?"

Some say you must give up all desire
and peace/God/knowledge/enlightenment
will settle upon you, a Divine dropped
mantle, rising with and following your breath.

One kind of meditation—
bringing the mind back kindly,
by the hand, from every thought
and image. Back to breath flow—
in and out, in and out.

Some leave everything and join
the monastery. There free from
worldly attempts to attain goods,
make a living, raise a family—
is time for contemplation, prayer.
Maybe God can be attained more quickly.

Sufis dance in the world, amidst it all,
embracing duties, company. Alone
in the crowd, remembering.

Some of the saints performed penances—

hair shirts that cut them,
flogging themselves to tear flesh, thorns.
Some received the stigmata—
wounds of Christ on hands and feet
bled on Friday.
Some fasted to receive visions.
Native Americans perform quests—
an animal comes to them,
gives them guidance.
It is God in some form.

Some use drugs: peyote, mescaline
to help make the sacred space.
Some force or being transports a message.

Mostly, we want to know
we are not alone here,
trying to navigate our way
through thumps, curves, smacking
and bursts of happy surprise.

My mother said singing
was nine times praying,
but I couldn't find my voice
in the wobbly high Catholic
Church Choir ladies, so I
sat on the organ bench turning
the sheet music for my cousin, Cathy.

Blessed are those with strong belief
who just know that God is there
surrounding them in all their endeavors.
Sad it is for those who feel they
must cram their God down other's throats.

As a child I memorized the Catechism.
Who made you?
God made me.
Why did God make you?
To know Him, to love Him, to serve

Him in this life and afterward in Heaven.
Nice answer. So clear.
I received it again at Rumi's Tomb
in Konya. "Know, love, serve God,"
said a voice, somewhere. Inside me?
"I will," I said, but there was no more.
The voice did not say how.
At Mary's house in Ephesus,
the message whispered was, "Be kind."

"Oh yes," I said. "I will, I'll try."
And I think gazing deeply into
the eyes of a loved one. Drinking in
all the world's beauty. Making art.
The rain of Grace. Maybe these are ways.

DECEMBER 1999
DEAR NATALIE,

I remember our walk one December years ago
through cornfields in the mild winter afternoon
in South Dakota where we met halfway. Fortune cookies
we asked for over and over until we got fortunes we liked.

You are many years divorced, a long string of your books
behind you on the shelf. I've only one (now at long last!);
but a grown son and a dear man who's here nightly
cleaning up the kitchen after I cook dinner.

I've been in India, you to Japan; but, there was nothing
like duck in plum sauce at Tremolo's in Paris,
our little room in the Jeanne d'Arc with sloping roof,
the train ride through fields of wild flowers to Italy,
and Naxos Island where we both had dysentery
but persisted in eating at the same friendly café.

France for you last time was a chunk of your leg
missing from a dog bite. Our home in Nebraska
caught fire and burned through to the outside.
Your father whose death you feared all these years
has done his passing. Both my dead parents
attend me in dreams.

You've gone on sitting and sitting on your Zen cushion.
Me, breathing and chanting my Sufi chants. Time
leaps and laughs like it's skipping ahead whole chapters.
We rarely phone or write; but, in this rainy drizzle
not yet turned to snow, I hold these recollections
tiny fragile birds perched on my open palm.

NEW YEAR'S DAY 2000
WHAT I LEAVE BEHIND

Our Shih tzu who fried herself in the car window
All the days our adolescent son was surly,
sneaked out, wouldn't speak
How my mother suffered with my leaving the church

I wouldn't mind leaving wrinkles
but I will carry them pressed
in my skin like a dried leaf
a wilted flower

All the memories
of things I didn't see
saw but didn't hold
held but clung to
until they made a groove
a ridge turned rigid

How my father's chest felt
like cement in his casket
I wanted to thump it
Beat out a rhythm
Wake him up one more time
Give him one more chance
to say he loved me

ABOUT THE POET

Barbara Schmitz grew up in Plattsmouth, Nebraska, where the Platte and Missouri rivers meet. Except for two years in California, she has lived on the plains and traveled to exotic, wonderful places including: Naxos, Greece; Ladekh and Kashmir, India; Konya, Turkey (to the tomb of the mystical poet, Rumi); Bali; and most recently Jerusalem and other parts of Israel. She has degrees from Wayne State College and the University of Nebraska at Omaha. She studied writing at Naropa Institute, where she was Allen Ginsberg's apprentice. She taught writing and literature at Northeast College in Norfolk, Neraska, for 30 years, and coordinated the Visiting Writer's Series there. Her chapbooks have been published by Sandhills and Suburban Wilderness presses. Her first full-length book, *How To Get Out of the Body*, was published by Sandhills Press in 1999. She and her husband Bob have one married son, Eli.